DATE DUE

THE
BLIMP
BOOK

Baron Wolman and Michael Wittman
present

THE BLIMP BOOK

Photography by
GEORGE HALL
and Baron Wolman

Text by
GEORGE LARSON

Design by
NEIL SHAKERY

SQUAREBOOKS
Mill Valley, California

Published by Baron Wolman/SQUAREBOOKS

Photographs copyright © 1977 by George Hall and Baron Wolman

Text copyright © 1977 by George Larson

Library of Congress Catalog Card Number 76-55590

ISBN (hardbound): 0-916290-04-2
ISBN (softbound): 0-916290-05-0

Printing by Cal Central Press, Sacramento, CA

Color Separations by Color Tech, Redwood City, CA

SQUAREBOOKS, Inc.
Post Office Box 144
Mill Valley, CA 94941

Printed in the United States of America

With heartfelt thanks to
the pilots and crews of the airships
America, Columbia, Mayflower, and *Europa,*
we dedicate this book to
those who truly sail the skies.

Very few people in the United States have never seen a blimp. Although some parts of the country are out of a blimp's reach, its image has been so extensively televised that it has become America's flying mascot. Goodyear's fleet of blimps has been flying around the United States since the 1920s, and since that time, millions of people have come to cherish the vision of the silver ships that float in the air.

Blimps are enchanting but remote, a source of wonder seldom satisfied by an opportunity to get close to the real thing. Strangely enough, even the people who haven't experienced the blimp at first hand seem to feel affection for it, and what's even more extraordinary, they form strong ideas, often misconceptions, about the structure and design of it and how it operates. Our book has been assembled not only to answer the hundreds of questions that bubble up around the blimps, but also to celebrate the benign beauty and grace of these delightful machines.

The idea for *The Blimp Book* began when George Hall, an experienced aviation photographer, was assigned by *Oui* magazine to shoot a story (unrelated to the blimp) in an area where the *Mayflower* was flying. He lucked into a ride, all but forgot about the original assignment and decided then and there to produce a book of photographs of blimps: blimps flying, blimps in repose, and the blimp's eye view of things. That was in 1972, and in the four years since then, he has accompanied the Goodyear fleet across America and Europe, recording with his camera the startling beauty of these airships. Aboard the blimps, he also became aware of the unique perspective afforded from the slowly passing balcony of the gondola, and a sampling of these aerial landscapes is contained here as well.

Hall's inspiration persuaded me and Baron Wolman, who produced this book, to join him in the project. We never had to wonder where to find the material, for there would be only one source — the four Goodyear airships. As we pursued the Great Fat Fleet to gather photographs and material for the book, we came to know the men who make up the crews as well as their families and friends. It's an astonishing group: in their way they're the most accessible, articulate people on the subject of their occupation (and preoccupation) to be found in any trade anywhere. There is a certain zany atmosphere that prevails in the family; to an inexperienced outsider, it occasionally appears as if everyone has been sniffing too much helium. As we recall our own strong feelings for the blimps, it's clear we've become a little crazy ourselves.

Since there are almost two hundred people working on the Goodyear blimps, it is impossible for us to extend our thanks to each who lent his or her help. Instead, we dedicate our book to them all, and we hope they'll accept this product of their spirited assistance.

There are several people, however, without whom the blimp project never would have left the ground. Bob Lane, for having had the courage and foresight to preserve the blimps for now and for the future when those about him were all too willing to deflate them permanently, deserves not just our thanks but everyone's. Tom Allison, Hank Nettling, Tom Riley and Frank Hogan of Goodyear's home office in Akron lent us invaluable access to company records and insights that have, almost in entirety, found their way into these pages. Without their help we would have had a far thinner story to tell. Moe O'Reilly, Dick Sailer and Terry Elms of Goodyear International helped us arrange tours with the *Europa*; we are deeply grateful for their efforts.

For their unstinting support and encouragement, we wish to express our special thanks to Calvin Bentsen, Vannie Cook and Mickey Wittman. And to Candace, Valarie and Juliana, we would return twofold the love, generosity and patience extended us during the creation of this book.

The project has been a unique joy, and we are delighted for the opportunity to share it with you.
GEORGE LARSON

1
BEHOLD
THE
BLIMP!

Of all the flying machines devised by man, only blimps seem somehow touched with divinity. Heavier-than-air craft are all commotion and bluster next to the serenity of a blimp. Even from a great distance, the sight of a blimp can transfix the senses and grip the imagination like some intruding but welcome apparition.

Its nature is contradictory. It is huge, yet insubstantial. It is the very shape of speed, yet it trundles through the air like a skyborne hippo, slowly, vulnerably. The shiny metallic envelope, seemingly a polished, monomorphic dart, is in reality a thin membrane, an undulating bladder swollen with the effort of containing the restless gases within. Beneath this great bag, like a remora on a shark, hangs the parasitic car. It dangles like an afterthought, yet it is the blimp's sole resident cargo. At the helm, a flyspeck of a human lends it intelligence. All that immense volume dedicated to so little living space!

The blimp's singular talent — its ability to hover without motion in utter ignorance of gravity — is an infinite resource requiring only the direction of a hand. A blimp provides the flight of dreams, the buoyant and effortless floating we encounter in the vague half slumber of dawn. Its unhurried plodding, as it noses to earth here and there like some mammoth bottom feeder, betokens a patience that is not of this frenetic world. A blimp might have issued from some alien intelligence, so out of step are its rhythms with our customary bustle. Its purpose seems at once mysterious and profound as it overlooks the aimless haste below.

Blimps exist today primarily to make people happy, and few other mechanisms are as successful in the execution of their purpose. But blimps evoke more than mere pleasure. These great tumid vessels have a unique allure. They induce a wild affection, and people who fall under their spell find themselves wishing somehow to embrace them.

Blimps have moods. For the most part they seem to carry themselves with a certain gentle humor tinged with melancholy. They wander like so many grey eternal ghosts. They rise above the gloom at dusk to glow in the sun's fire. At night, they loom in opaque skies, like unseen phantoms bearing all our fears. Attracting the most innocent of children and the weariest of grownups, they promise in their shadows relief from care and trouble. A blimp is pure fun, devoid of evil purpose. It has no natural adversary. It is an anachronism, stretching out its glory, playing a role that has no conceivable end while the riddle of its allure remains unanswered. Its future can be measured not by the life expectancy of its moving parts but by the need to have it around, and that may last forever. Nobody doesn't love a blimp.

The blimp's role as serious transportation has been almost forgotten. The great rigid airships of the twenties and thirties — the zeppelins — were the only lighter-than-air craft to succeed as transports. They were the ultimate expression of airship design, but they were as different from blimps as skyscrapers are from circus tents. The shape of a rigid airship was defined by a metal lattice frame covered with fabric, whereas the blimp owes its form only to the pressure of the gas within the envelope and the shape of the bag itself.

The principle upon which all lighter-than-air craft operate is as valid today as it was in their heyday. Whereas all heavier-than-air craft — airplanes, helicopters, autogyros, sailplanes — need motion to produce the lift necessary to keep them airborne, the blimp, or any dirigible, does not. Lighter-than-air craft obtain lift from natural buoyancy: a light gas (in the blimps' case, helium) contained in a bag displaces a large volume of heavier gas (the atmosphere) in order to produce a net weight gain equal to the difference in weight between the volume of atmosphere being displaced and the equal volume of helium contained within the bag. This gain can be put to work lifting things without using a drop of fuel. While an airplane in flight loses much of its driving energy to the induced drag resulting from the generation of lift by its wings, a blimp can use almost all of its motive power in simple forward or reverse motion. (Yes, blimps can back up.) A small fraction of the blimp's motion may go to the production of dynamic lift, but its ability to remain aloft without consuming energy makes the blimp remarkably fuel-efficient, a talent which

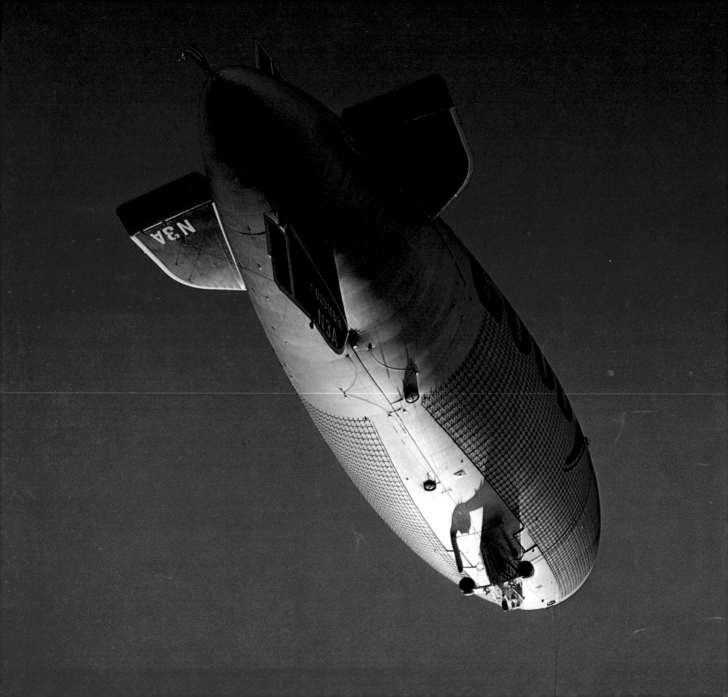

has led to recurring flurries of interest in reviving airships for transportation.

Modern blimps could operate for a week on the amount of fuel a jumbo jet uses taxiing from the terminal to the runway. A U.S. Navy blimp once set an endurance record by flying for eleven days and 9,000 miles without refueling, and the gigantic Hindenberg regularly crossed the Atlantic fully loaded on about five-hundred-dollars' worth of diesel fuel. But lighter-than-air craft have a practical maximum speed of 120 miles per hour. You can't have everything.

Although blimps are the only controllable lighter-than-air craft

flying today (balloons are lighter than air, but they drift in the wind with no lateral control whatsoever), they represent only one of three ways to design a dirigible. The word "dirigible" (from the Latin *dirigere,* "to direct") defines all airships that are engine-driven and steerable. All airships are dirigibles and all dirigibles are airships. All blimps are dirigibles, but not all dirigibles are blimps.

Rigid airships may also correctly be called "zeppelins," but no blimp can be a zeppelin, for a blimp is nonrigid. There are no rigid airships still operating, and although semirigid airships also once existed,

they too have passed from the scene. A semirigid airship had a frame that ran the length of the envelope along the bottom; this keel was its only rigid structure. The remainder of the hull was a bag attached to the keel, and the bag took shape only as it filled with gas. The sole solid structure on a blimp is the gondola or car, which is suspended by cables from the bag itself.

The blimps flying today are not all that large, as blimps go. The Navy once had a nonrigid called the ZPG-3W that was ten times the size of today's blimps; the volume of the Hindenberg was more than thirty times as large.

The origin of the word "blimp" has been the source of interminable argument. That "blimp" was a contraction of a British craft called a "balloon, type B, limp," has been discounted following the discovery that no such craft ever existed. So we are stuck with A.D. Cunningham and his playful thumb.

It is said that Cunningham, the commanding officer of a British air station at Capel, was conducting an inspection tour in 1915 and happened to snap his thumb against the fabric envelope of the SS-12, a nonrigid airship stationed there. The story goes that Commander Cunningham felt compelled, for reasons that are obscure, to imitate the sound he'd just made.

"Blimp!" said Cunningham.

So "blimp" it is.

The only company that has continued to produce and operate blimps is the Goodyear Tire & Rubber Company of Akron, Ohio. Aside from that fact that it manufactures the rubberized fabric of which blimp envelopes are made, Goodyear's reason for keeping its blimps flying was the discovery that the blimps are the most effective means it has for emblazoning its name in the public eye.

Goodyear has built more than 300 airships, most of them for the armed forces. The Navy formally decommissioned the last military blimp in 1964, and now Goodyear conducts blimp operations with four airships: the *Mayflower,* the oldest design and the smallest; the *Columbia* and *America,* both of newer design; and the *Europa,* commissioned recently and identical to the *Columbia* and *America.* The *Europa* operates in Europe, and it is the sole exception to the rule that blimps be named after yachts which have been victorious in various America's Cup races. That rule was established by P.W. Litchfield, a former president of Goodyear and a proponent of the idea that airships would one day fulfill the role of "air yachts" for residents of inland areas. That dream never came to pass, but the precedent of naming blimps after sailing champions has become traditional.

Where lighter-than-air ships once connected continents, roaming the ocean of air as the sovereigns of all vessels, we are left now with only the four Goodyear blimps and a couple of independently owned nonrigid airships. The blimps are a far cry from their revenue-earning, scheduled-carrier forebears, and their duties seem all frivolity by comparison. But even if they fly on as the final expression of an idea that now seems part of the past, the blimps endure. They survive. They are as permanent as the law of nature that buoys them. They are as eternal as whimsy. And if you should free your imagination for just a moment, you might fleetingly believe they are alive.

PONY BLIMP

FIRST 5 GOODYEAR CORDS MADE IN L.A.
FOR Douglass Fairbank's National Sextet
SOLD BY GARDEN COURT GARAGE & MOTOR SUPPLY CO.
7030 HOLLYWOOD BLVD.

2
GETTING OFF THE GROUND

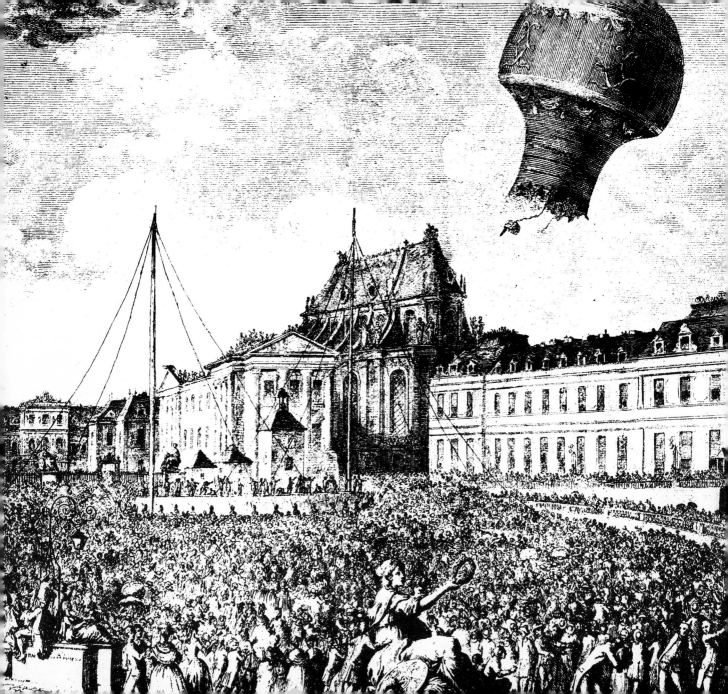

Humans have dreamed of flying since the earliest days of rational thought, but history and mythology are replete with failed attempts. While some involved machinery that went so far as to emulate the flapping of a bird's wings, the first giddy success in navigating the uncharted skies would ultimately come from a totally different source.

About 120 years before the Wright brothers' powered flights, another pair of aeronautically minded brothers, Joseph and Etienne Montgolfier of France, discovered a simple secret of flight: heated air trapped in a lightweight vessel, such as a paper bag, would lift the vessel and keep it aloft until the air cooled. Since the Montgolfiers were in the paper-making business, the brothers set about building a number of huge spherical paper balloons, each with a firepot suspended in a basket to keep the air hot. After several unmanned flights, the honor of being the first passengers in the air went to three unlikely candidates: a sheep, a duck, and a rooster. King Louis XVI and Marie Antoinette, both present at the launching from Versailles, had expressly forbidden any human cargo, fearing the venture to be dangerous in the extreme. The flight went perfectly, though, and the animals seemed completely unconcerned. With this success, the first manned flight was imminent. On November 21, 1783, scientist Pilatre de Rozier and the Marquis d'Arlandes climbed into the wicker basket and glided some five miles to a soft landing.

Within only two years, balloon flights covering 150 miles in six hours were not uncommon, and in 1785, Jean-Pierre Blanchard and the American Dr. Jeffries were carried by the wind across the English Channel. It was at this time that hydrogen was discovered (again by the Montgolfier brothers) to be a vastly more efficient lifting agent. Soon hydrogen-filled balloons were in military use as observation vehicles, and sport balloons were a common sight in Europe and America. But the new dream was of a powered balloon that could somehow be navigated at will, even against the wind. These improved machines were called dirigibles, and they enjoyed limited success during the mid-nineteenth century. Steam- and battery-powered electric motors were used to turn propellers. The powerplants were so enormously heavy relative to their power output, however, that these well-

intentioned ships could be utterly immobilized by a wind of only a few miles per hour.

It remained for one of the most engaging and remarkable men in the history of aviation, a Brazilian dandy named Alberto Santos-Dumont, to wed a dirigible to the newly invented, internal-combustion gasoline engine. The dapper little adventurer had been sent to Paris by his millionaire father with specific instructions to spend money and have a good time. Substantial amounts of those funds were spent on flying machines, and by the turn of the century he had become a common fixture in the skies above the French capital. Santos-Dumont built a total of fourteen gasoline-powered airships; he raced one around the Eiffel Tower to win a price of 100,000 francs (promptly donated to the city's poor) from industrialist and air-enthusiast Henry Deutsch de la Luerthe; in another, the tiny "No. 9", he frequently floated down to a landing in front of his favorite bistro on the Champs Elysees. When a beautiful young society girl, Mlle. Aida de Acosta, begged him for a ride, he gave her a quick lesson and sent her up alone. Santos-Dumont was convinced of the safety and the future of air travel, and he combined his efforts and fortune to promote the Age of Flight which he knew had arrived. Meanwhile in southern Germany, another dedicated nobleman, Count Ferdinand von Zeppelin, was about to capture the world's attention with the flight of a huge sausage-shaped gasbag that bore his name.

Left: Three farm animals ascend from Versailles. Center: Santos-Dumont with one of his small gasoline-powered dirigibles. Above: An early American balloon.

One warm July afternoon in 1900, thousands of curious on-lookers converged on the shores of Lake Constance near Friedrichshafen to watch the first flight of the Count's LZ-1, a 425-foot monster housed in a floating wooden hangar. The flight was short and the landing a controlled crash, but routine success was only a few years away. The zeppelins became a repository of national fervor, a role they enjoyed throughout their eventful forty-year history. Public subscriptions and donations from hundreds of thousands of Germans funded the Count's future successes. By 1910, only seven years after the first stumbling flight of the Wright brothers, huge hydrogen-filled zeppelins were plying scheduled passenger routes between major cities in Germany.

With the menace of war approaching, the Kaiser and his generals were quick to recognize the potential of Count von Zeppelin's invention as a powerful strategic weapon. Zeppelins were ultimately used as

Count Ferdinand von Zeppelin, and a Lake Constance test flight of one of his first rigid airships.

high-altitude bombers, despite von Zeppelin's reluctance, by the Imperial German armed forces during World War I, and in a conflict characterized by horrible new devices of death, none had greater psychological impact on the civilian populace. These great ships came over by night, flying so high that they could scarcely be seen or heard, out of range of conventional airplanes and antiaircraft guns. The actual

damage they caused was minimal, due primarily to the difficulties of night navigation and constant breakdowns in the thin, cold air. Nevertheless, they terrified the populations of London and the Industrial Midlands and greatly advanced the image of the ruthless and invincible Hun.

The later, more sophisticated wartime zeppelins were called "height climbers" because they were equipped with enormous gas cells and special Maybach engines that enabled them to cruise above England at altitudes of more than 20,000 feet. Airplanes of the day had great difficulty attaining even 12,000 feet; antiaircraft artillery had a similar vertical range. British aviators knew that just a single incendiary or tracer bullet entering one of the zeppelin's hydrogen gas cells would burn the huge ship in seconds, so the British equipped several airplanes with more powerful engines to close the altitude gap. The inevitable happened on the night of August 5, 1918, when a Rolls-Royce-powered DH-5 caught the new German L-70 at the uncharacteristically low altitude of 16,500 feet. Burning machine gun bullets found their mark, and the ship crashed with the loss of all hands, including Fregattenkapitän Peter Strasser, the charismatic and dynamic leader of the Imperial Navy's airship service. The incident demonstrated the vulnerability of the zeppelins, and military raids over England were soon suspended. However, the operation of more than a hundred rigid airships during the war years, often in unimaginably dreadful weather conditions, had created an invaluable pool of German experience and talent — thousands of captain, crewmen, riggers, engineers, and mechanics — that would keep Germany in the forefront of lighter-than-air technology for many decades.

Germany's defeat in the Great War led to crushing armistice terms which included the destruction of the Zeppelin company and its facilities at Friedrichshafen. In an effort to prevent the achievements of Count von Zeppelin from passing into oblivion, the Goodyear Tire & Rubber Company entered into an agreement with Dr. Hugo Eckener, a brilliant scientist who had assumed leadership of the Zeppelin organization after the Count's death in 1917. Goodyear bought key zeppelin patents and incorporated a new subsidiary, the Goodyear-Zeppelin Corporation. Goodyear had built nonrigid airships and tethered barrage balloons since 1911; now it added the world's foremost experts and technology to its new lighter-than-air division, including Dr. Karl Arnstein, chief engineer of Luftschiffbau-Zeppelin during its wartime construction of some seventy rigids. The U.S. Navy wanted a fleet of modern dirigibles second to none in design and capabilities, and awarded Goodyear-Zeppelin the contract for its first two ships.

In Europe, the Armistice Commission fortunately never carried out its threat to dismantle *Luftschiffbau-Zeppelin*. The company was, however, required to build several ships as reparations for the victors and from this program the U.S. Navy acquired the LZ-126, which it rechristened the U.S.S. *Los Angeles*. The Germans then set to work on the LZ-127, destined to become the most famous airship of all time — the *Graf Zeppelin*.

From the start the *Graf* was designed to be a commercial passenger airship. Dr. Eckener envisioned a fleet of such ships providing rapid, comfortable service between Europe, America, the Far East, and South

The Graf Zeppelin in Los Angeles on its 1929 world-girdling flight. Note the relative size of the Goodyear blimp.

Christening ceremonies for the Navy dirigible USS Akron in the Goodyear-Zeppelin Air Dock, August 1931.

America. The Graf Zeppelin was to be the machine that would point the way for future travelers and investors. At 755 feet, it was the longest and largest airship yet built. Its first flight was in September 1928. Less than a year later it would stun the world — still reeling from Lindbergh's solo Atlantic flight of 1927 — by flying around the earth with a full load of passengers and with only three stops, in Tokyo, Los Angeles, and New York. This amazing ship then settled into the routine it followed for several years, making scheduled round trips between Germany and Brazil. In flight, the *Graf* averaged over seventy miles per hour while the passengers dined regally, retired to their attractive staterooms, or stood at wide promenade windows which could be opened en route for better enjoyment of the land and seascapes passing a thousand feet below.

While the magnificent *Graf Zeppelin* was commanding international headlines in the late twenties and early thirties, the U.S. Navy was operating four of its own large rigids on training missions and maneuvers. The first Navy dirigible was the *Shenandoah,* American-built from German plans captured during World War I; the second was the German-built *Los Angeles,* delivered in 1924, in an historic transatlantic flight by Dr. Eckener himself; the third and fourth were the spectacular Goodyear-manufactured sister ships, the *Akron* and the *Macon.* All of the U.S. dirigibles were filled with noncombustible helium, thus eliminating hydrogen-filled airships' horrifying vulnerability to fire. The U.S. ships were, however, victimized by the same relentless enemy which threatens all aircraft: violent weather.

American airshipmen, although full of zeal and optimism, lacked the countless hours of flying experience which enabled their German counterparts to cope so well with crisis. When the *Shenandoah* wandered into a Midwest thunderstorm in 1925, the long envelope was snapped in two like a foundering ship. The rear portion crashed to earth while the forward section, flown like a free balloon by the crewmen clinging to its torn structure, eventually came to rest in a farmyard. In 1933, the *Akron* ventured out into the kind of spring storm that should have kept the ship grounded in its Lakehurst, New Jersey, hangar. Unfortunately, Admiral William A. Moffett, the Navy's head airshipman, had a fervent desire to show off the ship's all-weather capability, and the *Akron* took off into the storm, only to crash shortly thereafter in the Atlantic. Seventy-two men, including Moffett, were lost in aviation's worst disaster to that date.

The *Macon* went down in the Pacific two years later, succumbing to a fatal combination of rough weather and some previous structural damage that had been only temporarily repaired.

The Akron and its identical sister ship, the Macon, held nearly 7,000,000 cubic feet of helium within their 785-foot hulls.

Fortunately, lifesaving drills had been stepped up after the *Akron* catastrophe, and all but two of the *Macon's* crew were rescued. The loss of the *Akron* and *Macon* gave airship opponents an opportunity for protest, and the dirigibles were thoroughly castigated by press and military leaders alike as being useless as weapons of war.

In 1936, a new and much larger German zeppelin was put into commercial service. Christened the *Hindenberg,* the 804-foot behemoth was placed in scheduled passenger service between Germany and New York. The ship was far more elegant than the *Graf,* carrying seventy passengers in airborne luxury unequalled to this day. Since the war, the German ships had had an umblemished safety record. The decision was nevertheless made to replace the unstable hydrogen with helium, an inert lifting gas that would not burn. The Nazis were now in control of Germany, however, and the prospect of war was unmistakably arising again in Europe, America therefore refused to sell Germany the helium for the *Hindenberg,* fearing some future military use might be made of the gas. At the time, the United States held virtually all of the world's helium supply, so the Germans had no choice but to use hydrogen in their new ship.

On the evening of May 6, 1937, as the *Hindenberg* was making a routine landing at Lakehurst after a flight from Germany, fire suddenly broke out near the tail. In seconds, the entire length of the ship was settling to the ground in flames. Newsreel cameras, routinely on hand for zeppelin landings, recorded the catastrophe in gruesome detail. Thirty-six people, died in the holocaust. Although anti-Nazi sabotage has long been presumed to have caused the crash, no conclusive evidence has ever been uncovered to explain exactly what went wrong.

The loss of the Hindenberg effectively ended the dream of globe-gliding commercial airship service, perhaps forever. The *Graf Zeppelin,* on a return trip from Brazil at the time of the disaster, was put into the Friedrichshafen hangar upon its arrival and never flew paying passengers again. A newly completed sister ship to the *Hindenberg,* the *Graf Zeppelin II,* made a number of flights over Germany in the late thirties, but when World War II broke out, both ships were unceremoniously dismantled to make other use of their valuable aluminum.

Goodyear's experience with airships during this period went beyond their construction of the Navy rigids. The company had built military blimps during World War I, and in 1925 the first of Goodyear's commercial blimp fleet, the little *Pilgrim,* was test flown. The bag was filled with 47,000 cubic feet of helium, enabling the ship to carry two passengers plus the pilot. In 1928 and 1929, four larger ships, the *Puritan,* the *Vigilant,* the *Mayflower,* and the *Volunteer,* emerged from the Goodyear-Zeppelin shops; all were able to carry six passengers (as do the Goodyear blimps of today). A larger ship, the ten-passenger *Defender,* was also launched in 1929. Goodyear's president at the time, P.W. Litchfield, was a staunch believer in the future of lighter-than-air craft and he was

Left: Goodyear blimp pilots pose with their tiny Pilgrim in 1930. Right: A formation of Navy "L"-class training ships in 1944.

one of the key figures involved in the decision to mount a fleet of Goodyear blimps that would demonstrate the varied capabilities of nonrigid airships, while simultaneously carrying the Goodyear name across the country. The company set up a public-relations operation to extole the feats of the Goodyear blimps, which set out in all directions from Akron and soon became fixtures in the American sky.

The Goodyear blimps of the twenties and thirties differed little from today's ships. They carried the same payloads, had similar range and speed, traveled on similar tours, and even looked very much the same. The modern ships are made of tougher materials and their engines and instruments are more current, but otherwise their capabilities are almost unchanged. Few other aircraft, with the exception of some stunt planes and crop-dusters, compare as closely to their predecessors of forty years ago.

In the grim days following Pearl Harbor, Goodyear-Zeppelin, along with the whole of American industry, shifted totally to war production. The Goodyear blimps were repainted and turned into Navy trainers, their crews joining the Naval Airship Service almost to a man. During the war Goodyear built over 200 nonrigid airships for the Navy, most of them destined for use as anti-submarine convoy patrol craft. The blimps were among the most successful weapons of World War II; not a single ship was ever sunk in a convoy guarded by blimps. One Navy blimp was lost to enemy fire when it happened upon a German submarine disabled on the surface. The overly zealous blimp tried to press the attack, but the U-boat's machine guns peppered the airship so full of holes that it settled helplessly into the water. The sub was later sunk by surface ships.

Proponents of lighter-than-air craft tried to maintain their position in the postwar Navy, but it was a lost cause. Goodyear built a number of sophisticated nonrigid ships in the fifties. One of them, an enormous ZPG-2W, won the Harmon Trophy for the world's longest unrefueled flight. The record of 264 hours, or eleven days, still stands. The even larger ZPG-3Ws, 403 feet long and containing over one and a half million cubic feet of helium, were then and are still the largest nonrigids ever built. They carried a crew of twenty-five, and a revolving radar antenna, enclosed within the envelope, formed part of the nation's Distant Early Warning network over the Atlantic. The last of these blimps, undoubtedly the most advanced airship ever built, was decommissioned in 1962, and the Navy's Airship Service was no more.

Goodyear resumed commercial airship tours after the war, but the operation lacked impetus and dwindled into relative insignificance. In the early sixties when the only remaining Goodyear blimp was threatened with extinction, the program was revived by Robert Lane, the company's newly appointed public-relations chief. He took over the operation of the sole surviving *Mayflower* and immediately shipped it out on a strenuous road tour that was reminiscent of the blimp odysseys of the thirties. A second ship, the *Columbia,* was assigned to Los Angeles shortly thereafter. In 1969, a modern base and hangar were built in booming Houston to accommodate a larger computer-designed blimp, the *America.* This new 192-foot ship was filled with over 200,000 cubic feet of helium, and it sported a much-enlarged four-color electric night. A fourth Goodyear blimp, identical to the *America,* was assembled in England for operations in Western Europe. This ship, named the *Europa,* was based in Capena, Italy, a short distance north of Rome. A multinational crew was hired, and it trained with the U.S.-based ships before embarking on an American-style barnstorming tour of the Continent. The Goodyear blimps enjoyed a degree of public exposure never before achieved, particularly with expanded night-sign flights and television broadcasting missions being added to their many past accomplishments.

Since the tiny *Pilgrim* took its first excited guests aloft over a half century ago, the Goodyear blimp fleet has logged almost 200,000 hours in the air, flown over six million miles, and carried more than one million guests — all without a single passenger injury. And if Goodyear has its way, their gaggle of friendly gasbags will be flying for years to come.

Two modern Goodyear blimps in the Houston hangar.

3

CLOSEUP:
HOW
IT WORKS

This fascinating machine called a blimp is both simple and complex: simple in principle, complex in its refinement. It is the outgrowth of an intriguing natural phenomenon — that a bag filled with gas lighter than the surrounding air will rise and float across the land.

The earliest balloons used heated air as their light gas. Today's hot-air balloons employ the same technique, though bags are now made of strong synthetic fabrics and propane burners have replaced firepots as air heaters.

German zeppelins obtained their lift from millions of cubic feet of hydrogen, the lightest and most plentiful element in the universe. Yet despite its abundance, hydrogen is unstable to the point of violence. It needs only a spark in the presence of air to touch off the type of explosion and terrifying fire that ended the career of the *Hindenberg* and terminated the shining promise of the zepps themselves.

The Goodyear blimps use helium, a gas that is so slightly heavier than hydrogen that the difference is hard to measure. Helium is one of a family of elements called inert gases; do anything you like to helium, you'll get no bang, no fire, no nothing. It is comforting to know that riding above the gondola of the blimp is one of the world's safest known substances. Quite literally, *nothing* can happen to helium.

Helium is found primarily in the United States in certain deposits of natural gas located mainly in Texas and Kansas. Since it won't burn, the gas companies sepa-

Inflation of a new envelope takes about two hours. The ballast net holds the bag down until the gondola and fins are attached to add required weight.

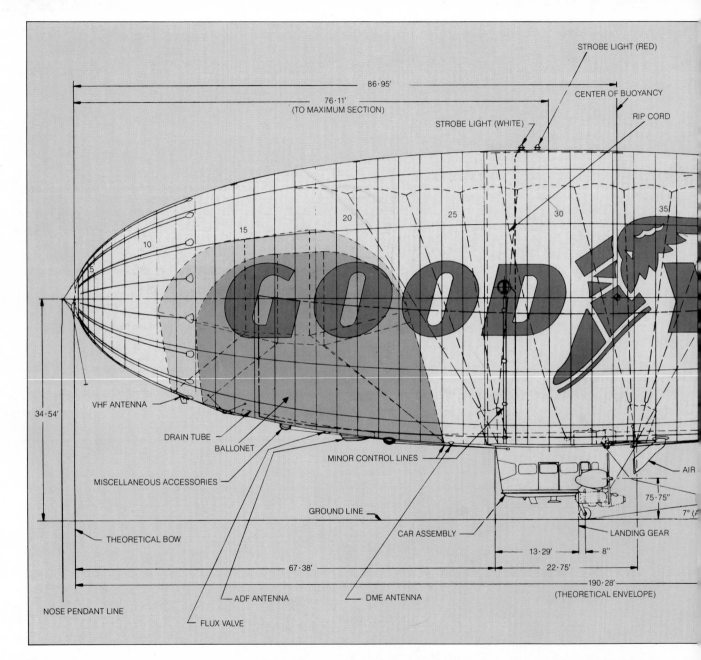

STROBE LIGHT (RED)

CENTER OF BUOYANCY

86·95'

RIP CORD

76·11'
(TO MAXIMUM SECTION)

STROBE LIGHT (WHITE)

35

30

25

20

15

10

5

GOOD

34·54'

VHF ANTENNA

DRAIN TUBE

BALLONET

MINOR CONTROL LINES

MISCELLANEOUS ACCESSORIES

AIR

75·75'

GROUND LINE

7° (A

CAR ASSEMBLY

LANDING GEAR

THEORETICAL BOW

13·29'

8''

22·75'

67·38'

190·28'
(THEORETICAL ENVELOPE)

NOSE PENDANT LINE

ADF ANTENNA

DME ANTENNA

FLUX VALVE

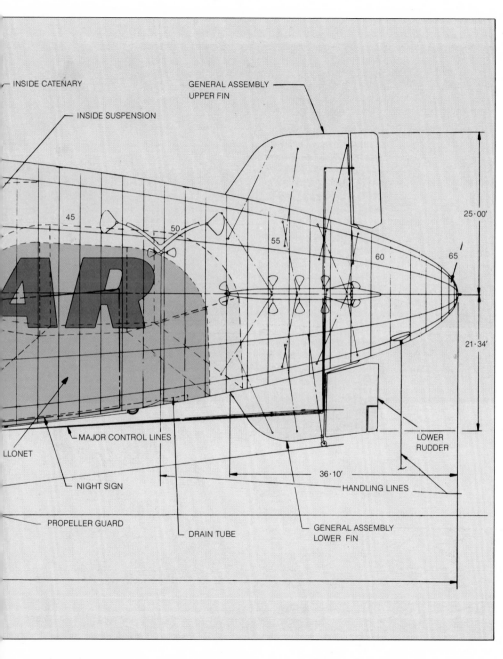

INSIDE CATENARY

GENERAL ASSEMBLY
UPPER FIN

INSIDE SUSPENSION

45

50

55

60

65

25·00'

21·34'

A R

LLONET

MAJOR CONTROL LINES

NIGHT SIGN

PROPELLER GUARD

DRAIN TUBE

GENERAL ASSEMBLY
LOWER FIN

36·10'

HANDLING LINES

LOWER
RUDDER

rate the helium from the flammable gas that's piped out to customers. To the gas companies, helium is merely an annoying impurity; to an airship, it's the breath of life. The larger Goodyear airships — the *Columbia,* the *America,* and the *Europa* — are each filled with more than 200,000 cubic feet of this rare gas. This amount is sufficient to lift the blimp's own empty weight plus that of six passengers, a pilot, some fuel and a bit of ballast. The *Mayflower,* which displaces only about 150,000 cubic feet, has somewhat less lift than the others.

If blimps were simply balloons, free to float with the wind, there would be little for the pilot to worry about. Want to ascend? Drop ballast. Time to land? Valve off some gas. But costing as much as fifteen cents per cubic foot, helium is too expensive to vent into the air, so Goodyear employs another system for its blimps. Borrowing an idea from the era of the Montgolfier brothers, Goodyear uses two air chambers called *ballonets.* The ballonets are located in the forward and aft ends of the blimps, and their purpose is to expand and contract to compensate for the expansion and contraction of the helium that occupies the rest of the envelope. Two scoops behind the propellers provide the ballonets with air pressure; auxiliary electric blowers do the job when the blimp is moored. When the ballonets must vent some air, valves are opened to dump the excess pressure. Deflating the forward ballonet and inflating the aft one will trim the blimp by squeezing the helium forward, thus lifting the nose; pushing the helium back by reversing the process will lighten the tail. By monitoring the total inflation of both ballonets, the pilot can control the pressure of the helium itself. Thus, the blimp can fly up to about 3,000 feet and compensate for the expansion of the helium at the lower pressure at that altitude by simply allowing the ballonet to collapse. No helium need be vented, no expensive gas is lost.

Goodyear's blimps maintain their shape solely by means of the pressure within the bag, which is made of Dacron fabric coated with neoprene rubber. It doesn't take much pressure in the envelope — about enough to push back an inch and a half of water — and when it's fully inflated the envelope is tight, strong and wrinkle-free.

The gondola, the car hanging below the bag, looks as if it is somehow fastened to the bottom. In fact it hangs from the top of the envelope. A system of steel cables attaches the roof of the gondola to two *catenary curtains* sewn into the topmost fabric of the envelope. The horizontal fins work like the feathers on an arrow to control the blimp's direction of flight. They are anchored to the envelope at their bases and supported in position by guy wires. The elevators and rudders are mounted on trailing edges of the fins so that they can control the up-down, left-right movement of the blimp. Cables connect the elevators to a large wheel at the

pilot's right, and the rudders to two huge pedals that he controls with his feet as if he were pumping an old air-organ. Other cables run from the gondola to the various vents and dampers that control air in the ballonets.

Mounted to the red aluminum nose cone is a large ball like the

ones found on trailer hitches; this engages with latches on the mooring mast to anchor the blimp firmly. Behind the nose cone, hollow aluminum tubes radiate back within laces. These *battens* help to reinforce the nose, which has to take a lot of strain when the blimp is moored.

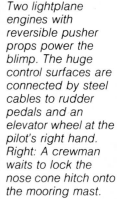

Two lightplane engines with reversible pusher props power the blimp. The huge control surfaces are connected by steel cables to rudder pedals and an elevator wheel at the pilot's right hand. Right: A crewman waits to lock the nose cone hitch onto the mooring mast.

A strong wind will actually elongate the blimp visibly, and you can watch the track of its single wheel change as the wind stretches the envelope.

The mast is designed to hold the blimp firm in hurricane-force winds, and it has successfully done so more than once. But should the ship somehow wrench itself free from the hitch, it won't go far. Sewn into the top of the envelope is a twenty-two-foot zipper-like device called a *rip panel*. This panel is connected by a rope to the top of the mast whenever the blimp is moored, so that the ship will tear itself open and deflate if it accidentally breaks away. This is a last-ditch emergency measure, and no crew member remembers seeing it used.

Goodyear manufactures the envelopes at a facility in Arizona, while the blimps themselves are assembled and inflated in the Houston hangar. A blimp has a life expectancy of about six years before the envelope will have aged to the point where it begins to leak helium. The cars have no limit to their useful lives. Most of them have actually been in service since World War II, though they are periodically stripped down and completely refurbished.

The blimp's two engines are similar to those found on typical lightplanes, except that they have been mounted backward to push instead of pull with their propellers. The props are reversible — a good thing, since they are the only way of stopping the blimp. There are no brakes!

The blimps cruise at about

thirty-five miles per hour, with a flat-out top speed a little over fifty. Of course, the wind has a lot to do with the ship's true speed. A thirty-five-mph headwind will stop the ship cold, and that same wind on the tail will send it galloping along at seventy. If they are flown economically, they can stay in the air for twenty-four hours on a full load of fuel. That might be a bit uncomfortable, however, since there are no rest rooms or kitchen facilities aboard.

The actual lift that helium is willing to produce on a given day

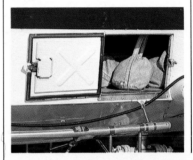

can be affected by as many variables as the stock market: temperature, atmospheric pressure, and altitude being only three variables in the equation.

Although the blimps are called "lighter-than-air" craft, they usually operate with enough ballast to make them slightly heavier than "EQ" (equilibrium, or zero weight). The blimp's forward motion through the air will produce enough dynamic lift to compensate for this heaviness. In fact, the Goodyear blimps can fly as much as 800 pounds heavy on the rare occasion, such as a long cross-country assignment, that calls for a lot of equipment and fuel. A truly heavy takeoff requires a rolling technique like that used by airplanes, with the blimp trundling painfully down the runway on its single wheel. When the ship is operating in its normal range, the typical takeoff weight is 100-200 pounds heavy, and the ship is usually tossed

A compartment at the rear of the car holds 25-pound shot bags for fine trim. Crewmen prepare to bounce the blimp on its wheel for an "up-ship" takeoff (right).

into the air — literally — by the crew. The pilot then advances the throttles and continues upward on momentum and thrust.

There's no great trick to estimating the heaviness or lightness of a blimp. A good rule of thumb is that for each pound in weight, the blimp will sink one foot per minute; therefore, 100 pounds heavy yields 100 feet per minute down. (If light, it will rise at the same rate.) An experienced crew chief can estimate a blimp's weight, or lack of it, by ordering

Crew chief gives hand signals to the pilot and the crew when guiding the blimp onto the mooring mast ("raise the nose;" "keep it coming;" "nose to the left").

his crew to raise the ship until the hand rail of the gondola is at shoulder height. When they let go he simply watches what happens. Shot bags, each containing twenty-five pounds of lead, are added or removed from a bin in the bottom of the gondola as the pilot and crew chief direct. Once they are satisfied with the ship's weight, the pilot signals the airshipman's traditional command to cast off — "Up ship!" — and the crew on the hand rail will lift the blimp once more, let it drop and bounce on its wheel, then heave it aloft like a huge medicine ball.

The blimp climbs at a startling angle, its engines roaring as it scrambles for altitude, usually about a thousand feet for cruising. Then the engines are throttled back and the airship levels and settles in for the flight. One odd thing about these airships is that they do everything — climb, cruise, dive — at the same speed: thirty-five miles per hour. Pilots of heavier-than-aircraft are usually startled by this wierd behavior, particularly the steep takeoff angle. Once accustomed to it, however, they can't stop smiling; no airplane can be handled with such abandon.

Landing is a more complex operation than takeoff. If the helium has heated and a lot of fuel has burned off, the blimp may be hundreds of pounds lighter than it was at takeoff. A light ship has no desire to land. It must be *driven* forcefully to the ground, nose down, engines thrashing away at high power, holding the unwilling beast to earth until the crew is able to hurl

enough ballast aboard to keep it down for good.

The most important factor on the approach is the direction of the wind, for the blimp must land *exactly* into it. Any amount of drift sideways makes the ground crew's job immeasurably more difficult. To assist the pilot in determining wind direction right up to the last moment, the crew chief holds up a small wind sock as the pilot aims the airship toward him. Two teams of three men are assigned to catch the trailing nose lines as the blimp nears the ground. They grab the ropes and run to the side, holding the nose into the wind, while the remainder of the crew rushes in to grasp the handrail on the gondola and load shot bags aboard. It looks like a fire drill, but it has purpose and method in its apparent madness. Blimps are the most helpless during landings, when crosswinds and gusts can roll them precariously. Oddly enough, calm days are no particular blessing, for with no wind whatsoever, the pilot's control is significantly lessened. The ideal condition is a steady ten-mph breeze, just enough to keep some air flowing over the rudders and elevators.

When flying operations are completed for the day, the blimp is walked to the mast by the crew, each member holding fast to the hand rail or a nose line. The huge ship is inched toward the locking cup atop the thirty-foot mast, where another crewman waits to wrestle the hitching ball into position and secure it. The crew chief, standing in front of the mast and craning his neck upward, orchestrates this delicate series of movements with a flourish of hand signals and shouted orders. Once the blimp is locked on and shut down, auxiliary electric blowers are placed on the two ballonet scoops to maintain proper envelope pressure as the restless helium cools and contracts. At least one crewman stays on watch after the others leave. The blimp is never left alone.

Even in repose, the blimp seems to have a life of its own. It tracks fitfully around the mast on its wheel as the breeze eddies and shifts. Occasionally the tail lifts gracefully into the air as wind currents bubble underneath the enormous fins. Automatic pressure sensors switch on the electric ballonet blowers from time to time, puffing outside air into the cells as the helium pressure slowly drops. Once an hour, the lone crewman on watch climbs into the car, sticks his head up into a sealed plexiglass bubble in the roof, and shines a flashlight at the two ballonets. A vertical column of numbers on each cell, like the plimsoll mark on the bow of a ship, enables him to read the degree of ballonet inflation. This information, recorded twenty-four times a day and 365 days a year, is supplemented with a daily check of helium purity. Taken together, they form a careful record of the envelope's inevitable aging process. About once a year, the blimp is attached to a mobile distilling machine which removes air and moisture from the helium and restores the gas to near one hundred percent purity.

The Goodyear crews have been flying their airships for more than fifty years, and by now they easily execute their routines to perfection. While simple in principle, these systems are complex in performance, but mastering the techniques of one of the most unusual jobs in the world offers a unique satisfaction.

Crewmen manhandle the two nose lines to keep the blimp pointed into the wind.

4

THE
ROAD
SHOW

oodyear has a very big problem. There are an awful lot of people to whom it has to say "no". It hurts to have to say it, but the three Goodyear blimps which tour America simply can't oblige the thousands of requests for their presence at this clambake and that county fair. The clambake and county fair are almost sure to be on the same day but several hundred miles away from each other. Blimps are wonderful machines, but after all, they only travel at thirty-five miles per hour. So scheduling for the three beauties occasionally means giving one event the nod and telling the other, "We'll be happy to try fitting it in next year."

The annual itinerary of each blimp is mind-boggling, an exercise in logistics and scheduling that would occupy the staff of a good-sized army. The company kept a close record of the 1976 summer tours for the three U.S. blimps. The results: the *Mayflower, America,* and *Columbia* covered a total of 120,000 air miles; at thirty-five miles per hour, that's 3,429 hours of in-transit flying, not counting the time spent on local flights at each town and event they visited. The three ships flew in twenty-eight states and touched eighty-three major cities during the fast-paced summer, and in the process 14,000 passengers were given rides. Goodyear estimated that by summer's end, some sixty million people had seen a blimp firsthand.

The season during which the blimps operate away from their bases begins in the spring and lasts approximately six months. The off-season is occupied primarily with maintenance, refurbishing, and local promotional efforts. The routes the blimps are to travel are carefully planned before the season begins in order to make optimum use of available time and to arrange transit flying in a logical

Overleaf: Televising pro football at the Los Angeles Coliseum. Left: The Mayflower graces the Houston skyline. Below: She "sails" up the East River in New York.

The big semi, the slowest vehicle, leads the caravan to the next stop. Navigator in the right seat keeps the group on course.

sequence, minimizing wasted trips and backtracking. Attendance at some events has become traditional. For instance, there's always a blimp on station at the Indianapolis 500 Memorial Day race, and the America's Cup yacht racing series is another must. Other stops on the tour, however, are unrelated to public events. They are just goodwill visits to increase popular awareness of the Goodyear name.

Due to the operational limitations of a blimp, certain areas of the country are out-of-bounds. The practical limit of the airships' flying altitude is around 3,000 feet, with an absolute maximum of 10,000 feet, so it's

The crew's clerk catches up on paperwork in the office inside the crew bus. Below, crewmen at work in the mobile machine shop. Suspended from above are auxiliary fuel tanks which are mounted on the airship for long cross-country flights.

obvious that cities such as Denver and Albuquerque are out of luck. At those locations, the blimp would be hard-pressed to lift its own weight, much less carry passengers or TV gear.

Flights between cities are usually made during daylight hours and normally average about 300 miles, or eight hours of flying. Two pilots share the flying duty, alternating in the left-side captain's chair every hour. The off-duty pilots travel with the ground crew in a rolling circus of vehicles which includes a bus, a small van, and a huge trailer truck with generators, spare parts, and machinery. Tagging along in this gypsy train are the private cars belonging to the families of the crew members. As many as twenty-three Goodyear employees may travel with a blimp, including five pilots, seventeen crewmen, and a public relations representative. These treks attending any intercity movement of a blimp have a sort of riotous organization to them. The PR man generally precedes the group by a couple of days, acting as combined advance man and scout. One crewman is appointed navigator. This individual leads the main group from the shotgun seat of the trailer truck, the slowest vehicle and therefore the logical pacesetter. The navigator is under pressure all the way: he dare not (1) get lost; (2) drive in such a way as to get the group broken up; or (3) miss meeting the blimp at the destination, because a blimp cannot land without a crew. Of course, no navigator is perfect, and there is

The crew pounds stakes, assembles the three-piece mast, and pulls it upright.

more than one horror story of part of a caravan barreling down the interstate, watching with appalled fascination as the other portion passes in the opposite direction.

Strange things can happen along the convoy's route. One Goodyear vehicle with the old yellow paint scheme was plagued by people who climbed into it at stoplights on the assumption that it was a taxicab. (These days the equipment sports a handsome blue-and-white scheme.) On another occasion, the pilots in the blimp tried to be helpful by directing the ground navigator along a short-cut to the airport. Things went swimmingly until the truck driver suddenly found himself having to back away from a too-low underpass that the pilots had failed to notice. The result was a two-hour traffic jam, naturally at the height of the rush hour, that did little to enhance Goodyear's public-relations image. Since then the pilots have left the driving to the drivers.

Usually it is not difficult for the ground procession to match or even exceed the blimp's moderate cross-country progress. After a morning takeoff, there is plenty of time to disassemble the mooring site, clean up and settle airport bills, hit the road, stop for lunch, and still make it to the next stop before the blimp gets there. The blimp and the ground vehicles are in regular contact with each other by radio, so there are few surprises. Upon arriving at the destination aerodrome, the crew immediately begins erecting the mooring mast. The mast

is made up of three sections fitted together end-to-end and then raised, like a tent pole, and guyed by staking cables.

When the blimp looms up over the horizon, an unspoken message always sweeps through the streets. Although nobody signals the citizenry, the folks somehow *know* the blimp is going to land at their town. And when the town is a small one like Tifton, Georgia,

or Zanesville, Ohio, the arrival is an event of major significance. By the time the blimp is on its final approach, wide-mouthed, wide-eyed gaggles of children and adults are elbow-to-elbow at the airport fence, mesmerized by the astonishing sights unfolding before them. Various "experts" can be heard murmuring completely erroneous data to gullible children, but neither truth nor numbers matter. It is the experience itself which counts. For years to come these people will talk about the day the blimp came to town.

In bigger cities, the crowd is every bit as large, every bit as susceptible. "Are they landing it? Are they letting it down?" "Yeah, uh, I think so. Yeah, there, see? See those ropes? That's the landing gear. They'll tie it down with those." There are a thousand explanations for the blimp's every move; the strangeness of it all compels one to say *something*,

As the blimp's cross-country trek continues, the crew stows the mast and boards the vehicles, en route to the next night's stop.

The thousands of bulbs that make up the night sign are controlled by electronic tapes programmed on a computer in Akron. The tape-transport and lamp-drivers replace the passenger seats for night flights, and a turbine power unit is hung beneath the car to provide the extra juice.

even conjuring up a fantasy or two.

Once the blimp is moored, the awe-struck crowd soon finds a way to approach it. It is an unwritten law of human nature as absolute as the love rites of spring: the blimp is there, therefore the people will come to it. The crew fends off the most aggressive in a friendly way, making certain that curiosity causes harm to neither person nor blimp. Eventually the crew climbs on the bus and heads for a motel near the airport, leaving one lone crew member to stand the night's first watch. Long after the summer dark has settled, he will be handing out pamphlets and answering the same questions with whatever energies he has left after a long day. Finally, the last youngster borne on the shoulders of the last adult will run out of things to ask and the crewman will turn to other duties — monitoring pressure, working on some equipment, keeping an ever-wary eye on the weather.

If the blimp has planned a stay of several days, passenger flights will be the main order of business. Rides on the Goodyear blimps are offered by company invitation only with Goodyear's district management office for the area controlling seat allotment. Most of the lucky riders are customers of Goodyear's various retail divisions, local dignitaries, and members of the press. Despite the airship's huge size, the small gondola can only hold six passengers plus the pilot — a surprise to those with visions of transoceanic zeppelin travel dancing in their heads. The ride

is usually a thirty-minute spin over the town and back, the pilot occasionally plunking a delighted passenger into the left seat for a try at steering the ship. After the flight the blimp returns to the airport and quickly exchanges its guests for another group while the ground crew

hangs onto the hand rails and nose lines. The ship is seldom on the ground more than a minute between flights.

On evenings when the blimp is assigned to fly a night-sign mission, the routine changes. The Super Skytacular night sign has its own set of equipment that must be installed and checked out before the flight begins. Mounted on the flank of each blimp are thousands of lights (actually automotive taillight bulbs covered with plastic discs colored red, yellow, blue, and green) which enable it to

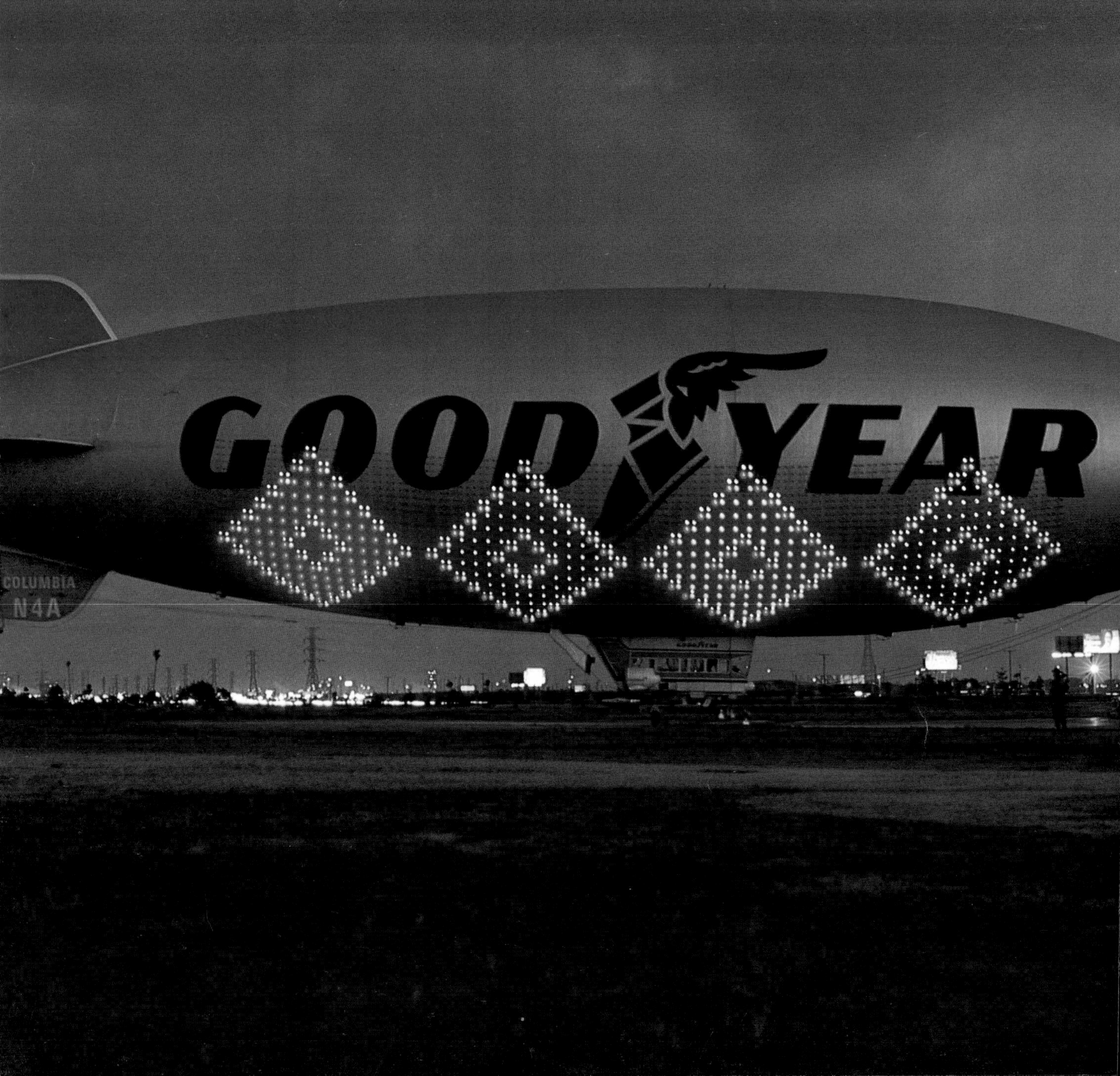
GOODYEAR
COLUMBIA
N4A

produce the images and words of the animated night-sign messages. Although the lights are permanently installed, the mechanism which reads the computer-programmed tapes is not. This must be put aboard in place of passenger seats, along with an externally mounted, auxiliary turbine-power unit to generate the additional electricity the lights require.

The night sign is an electronic marvel. In the early days, a blimp was wired to display only a single message at a time, but the present signs are computer-controlled super-whiz contrivances which produce the most complex images and effects of any lighted sign in the world. A computer at Goodyear Aerospace's Akron facility is programmed to allow a technician to design a message (in English or any other language; the Europa has "spoken" eight languages so far) and record it on a magnetic tape. The completed cassette is checked for correctness and then dispatched to each blimp for use. A trained technician goes aloft and operates a machine on the blimp that can read the tape and illuminate each one of the thousands of bulbs in precisely the correct sequence and for the proper length of time. When the sign first lights up at night, there is occasionally a concurrent light show at the switchboard of the local police station. To try to minimize this, one tape begins with the message: "IT'S NO UFO — JUST THE GOODYEAR BLIMP!" Although the night signs are used to promote the many Goodyear

The Super Skytacular night sign is capable of an infinite variety of four-color electronic designs: moving word messages, stick-man dramas, or psychedelic light shows.

products, most of its programming is of a public service nature. Non-profit events and charities are mentioned on the sign, in between dazzling four-color designs and animated cartoons. A typewriter keyboard is also part of the night-sign installation, and on it the technician can spell out messages directly onto the sign instead of playing the tape. For the past several years, the *Europa* has flown all night over the twenty-four-hour auto race at Le Mans, using its sign to broadcast position reports on the various cars vying for the lead.

A nother traditional role for the blimp stems from its marvelous ability to serve as a camera platform for photography or for television broadcasting. Goodyear makes advance arrangements with the television networks to provide the blimp for aerial coverage of public events. The company also supplies a lightweight color camera and on-board electronics, all specially modified for use in the blimp. The network or station need only send a cameraman and a video technician. A microwave transmitter sends the camera's signal from the blimp to a dish antenna and receiver on the ground; this signal can be fed live into the network or put on video tape for later broadcast or replay. The TV crewmen stay in constant contact with their director via a separate two-way radio link, to which the pilot also listens for positioning cues.

Different sports events require varying camera and piloting techniques. The low drone of the blimp's engines has been known

to irritate golfers and tennis players, so the standard operating procedures at Forest Hills or Pebble Beach is to keep well off to the side and let the camera's enormous Schneider 30:1 zoom lens close the gap. Football players and fans don't worry much about noise, however, so they see the blimp almost directly overhead. During coverage of a motorcycle race in California, one airborne cameraman took a lambasting from the director for failing to keep his camera trained on the leaders of the race. The man was not at

For network television assignments, the blimp is loaded down with a color camera and microwave transmission equipment. A cameraman and a technician join the pilot over the event. With doors and windows open, it is often uncomfortably chilly in the airship.

The Goodyear blimp is a well-known gatè-crasher at some of the greatest American spectacles; the Rose Bowl, the Bicentennial Parade of the Tall Ships, and the start of the Indianapolis 500 are only three of many such events.

fault, though; a stiff wind was blowing and the blimp, even though it was striving full steam ahead, was actually moving backwards.

The Goodyear blimps have appeared in a number of Hollywood productions, with roles in *Nashville, Once Is Not Enough, Two Minute Warning, A Star Is Born,* and the Beatles' film *Help!* among others. They never had a starring role, however, until a blimp was featured in Paramount's film version of the bestselling book *Black Sunday.* The plot centers around a Middle East terrorist scheme to commandeer the blimp and carry a plastic bomb over the Super Bowl game. Three blimps were used during the filming of various action sequences, and many of the blimp crew members and pilots appear in the film as well.

Goodyear also makes its airships available for a variety of scientific purposes. One was used as a flying wind tunnel in aerodynamic studies. By hanging test vehicles below the blimp, scientists were able to obtain accurate airflow data, unencumbered by confusing side effects that might have been caused by the walls of a common static wind tunnel. Another blimp was a target for sonic-boom experiments at Edwards Air Force Base in California. It hovered at 2,000 feet while jets flew past at supersonic speeds, aiming shock waves at measuring instruments on the airship. Pollution-monitoring equipment has often been carried aloft aboard the *Columbia* over Los Angeles, and the same ship has been used for urban-planning surveys and transportation studies.

One of the most fascinating, and oddly appropriate, uses to which the *Columbia* is put is in assisting members of the American Cetacean Society in their annual count of the California grey whale, which migrates along the Pacific Coast every winter. The whale-watch flights over the last decade, often at a low and lazy four knots corresponding to the whales' cruising speed, have revealed that the animals have stabilized their once-fragile population growth. In fact, recent indications are that other cetacean species are inhabiting the coastal waters in increasing numbers, possibly seeking refuge from the slaughter that continues in the Pacific.

After more than four decades of successful commercial airship operations all over America, Goodyear began in 1971 to assemble components for a fourth blimp which would hopefully generate similar excitement in Europe. In many ways, however, the European venture would have to differ from the U.S. oper-

Left: The Europa weighs off in a field near Munster, West Germany. Right: The medieval maze of Chartres, France.

ation. For one thing, the many national boundaries to be crossed, and the red tape which would attend each crossing, could make life infinitely more complex for a European crew than for their American counterparts. European countries are not very large in area, but bureaucratic barriers seem to stretch the intervening miles. Language was bound to be another problem, as would the innumerable filings and permissions which must accompany almost every private or corporate flight in European airspace. And in Europe everything simply could be expected to cost more.

First a hangar for the ship had to be built. Constructed in Capena, Italy, for $2.5 million, it's a modern and completely equipped facility that can service any need. While the Italian hangar was being readied, the components of the *Europa* were shipped to Cardington, England, for assembly at an airship hangar still maintained there by the Royal Aircraft Establishment. When the new *Europa* took off from the Cardington base, it was the first time an airship had flown over Britain in more than forty years. The last British-made airship had been the ill-starred R-101, which crashed tragically

in 1930 and ended England's desire to build others. After being test-flown, the *Europa* prepared to cross the Channel for its first tour of the Continent.

The crewmen of the *Europa* represent a variety of nationalities, ten countries in all. From the start the intention was for the American team which led the initial *Europa* crew, slowly to be replaced until the crew was made up entirely of native Europeans.

Most of the original European crew members had spent part of a tour season with one of the American ships before going to work in Europe, so they knew the basics of blimping from actual

experience rather than theory.

With the passage of time, the operation in Europe has become much smoother, as the various governments and their agencies become used to the comings and going of the *Europa*. The interminable border delays which marred the first tours — crewmen and customs officials haggling over such fine points as whether helium was being imported — have dissolved as the crossings become routine. Traffic controllers, bewildered at first by the bizarre American craft that tracked their radar screens at a crawl, now welcome the *Europa* into their airspace. To date, the ship has already flown within fourteen countries.

What better way could there be to view the delicate scale of Europe? Left: A Dutch windmill near Rotterdam and a patchwork of Belgian farms. Right: London's Thames River and the Houses of Parliament.

5

AMERICA'S SWEET-HEARTS

Not something you see every day: the America buzzes delighted pleasure-boaters on Long Island sound.

Every few years, an expert appears proclaiming, in print or on TV, the rebirth of airships. These short-lived media blitzes are carbon copies of one another. Most say in essence that airships are not artifacts of an irrelevant past but the touchstones of the future, that they were too far ahead of their time and that their ascendancy has now come. These stirrings of interest, as regular and inevitable as elections and taxes, usually generate a flurry of excitement among lighter-than-air proponents and a few others who are hearing it all for the first time. Another group, having heard it all before and having thought it invalid even then, responds by flatly panning the airship and anyone crazy enough to suggest it could replace anything. Goodyear, alone among the parties to this seasonal conflict, stays quietly aloof, for it alone knows the truth. To argue whether the blimp is efficient or inefficient, weather-resistant or hyper-vulnerable, fuel-saving or gas-greedy, pollution-free or messy, cost effective or wasteful, commercially viable or a certain loser, is simply missing the point.

The secret, which the blimps hold wrapped in mystery within their ethereal hulls, is that they embody some spirit, some intangible quality that sets them apart from ordinary experience and draws people to them. The people who serve on the Goodyear crews understand this perhaps better than anyone else, for they willingly abandon any semblance of a normal life when they sign on. Although each indi-

vidual may choose different words to describe what happens, they are saying essentially the same thing: they are hooked. They fly blimps because they have to. No substitute will do.

Cowboys are said to love their horses, but the machine age has brought with it a seemingly widespread and irreversible alienation from such affection. People talk about "loving" their cars, but it's not the same. No car ever brought its driver home by itself. Things made of metal and plastic may give pleasure by extending a person's power, by responding with great strength and sensitivity, like slaves to their operator's direction. However, the shared spirit of adventure between man and a living beast of burden has gone — with one lone, troublesome exception: the blimp. To attribute "life" to a blimp is to invite ridicule, but it well may be the only explanation for the peculiar quality of the human-blimp relationship.

Goodyear has no particular desire to construct blimps for a waiting world. Its airships are not for sale. It does not measure the success of its fleet of four in terms of profit or loss, pounds of freight lifted, or distance covered. The blimps exist simply to persuade people to feel kindly toward Goodyear, and as a recognizable image the blimps are unbeatable. A corporation the size of Goodyear does nothing by chance, so studies are made periodically to assess public sentiment toward the big silver gasbags. The results are not merely positive — they are almost hysterically favorable.

Master modeler Eddie Chavez with his scale model of the Columbia, now on display at the Smithsonian National Air and Space Museum.

Because the blimps tend to generate so much emotion and excitement, and also because few people are actually familiar with blimps and how they work, strange things often happen to the airships and their crews. One elderly passenger was surprised by the large wheel at the captain's right hand. This controls the elevators that direct the ship up and down, but nobody had explained it to her. When she demanded to be let off before the blimp even departed, the crew asked why. "I'm not flying with any pilot who's in a wheelchair," was her answer. It made perfectly good sense to her.

Most VIP's are very gracious and enjoy the ride when it's offered. Richard Petty, the NASCAR racing champion and a user of Goodyear's racing tires, spent the first few moments of his flight searching for his seat belt before he realized he didn't need one. (The Goodyear blimps are the only powered aircraft which are certified for flight without seat belts.) Dwight D. Eisenhower is said to have dropped what he was doing at the approach of a blimp, accepting with childish enthusiasm the crew's invitation for a ride. A week later, the crew got a note of thanks from the former president, a newly converted lighter-than-air fan.

Other big-shots have been less pleasant. Blimp passenger flights for Goodyear's friends and invited guests are very tightly scheduled, in order to minimize time and handling on the ground. Passengers are asked to be at the departure airport well ahead of their scheduled takeoff because it is undesirable to have the blimp tarrying in the grip of the ground crew. The crew doesn't like it, and neither does the blimp. A well-known United States senator was invited for a ride with his grandson, but they arrived late. As the disappointed boy watched the departing blimp grow smaller in the distance, his famous grandfather tried to bring the weight of his office to bear on the crew. Like any grandparent, the senator was loathe to face an unhappy child, and the crew's explanations about on-time operations got nowhere.

"That's all well and good," thundered the senator, "but *you* explain to the boy why he can't have a blimp ride."

One of the blimp pilots looked at the boy, smiled, and said simply, "I'm sorry, but you won't be able to have a blimp ride because your grandfather was late."

In 1968, the blimp covering the Sebring Twelve-Hour Race in Florida had to divert from its TV role to assist law enforcement officials in rounding up a fugitive. The fleeing felon was ultimately spotted running through the woods. One can only imagine what went through his mind when he looked up and saw what was making all that racket overhead.

Air show fans loll beneath the Columbia at Abbotsford, British Columbia.

Explaining his capture-by-blimp to his cellmates must have been even worse.

At the same auto race, the Goodyear Racing Division staff was worried about the impending weather. "Why not check with the blimp people? They're weather experts; they have to be," it was suggested. So the tire engineers asked the blimpos to watch the weather, and for twenty-four hours they observed and measured, discussed and evaluated. The decision: rain, and lots of it. Definitely. No question about it. The Racing Division's tire busters went to work, mounting rain tires for all its customers. Ultimately, the race was the warmest and sunniest ever. Not a drop of rain.

Then there are all those crazy schemes people keep coming up with. One millionaire wanted to hire a blimp to hoist his yacht out of a landlocked lake and drop it into the Gulf of Mexico. Another fellow, explaining he was an advertising executive on the West Coast, phoned to say he wanted to buy an airship so he could paint it to look like a pineapple. He also wanted to rent one of Goodyear's hangars, painting *that* to look like a pineapple can. His plan: to photograph the pineapple flying in and out of the can. You couldn't fault the guy for thinking too small, but the price took his breath away.

The blimp crew sometimes has to fight its own popularity. One of the crews arrived at the entrance to their assigned motel only to find a note tacked to the door: "Back at 6 o'clock. Gone to air-

port to see blimp."

Nude bathers at Black's Beach in La Jolla, California, complained not about prying eyes from the occasional blimp's passing gondola but about the huge shadow it cast. They claimed that until the blimp passed and the sun came back

out, they froze half to death.

Two nuns once swore they saw a blimp land inside a football stadium, something no blimp has ever done. A woman insisted to authorities that a blimp had landed in her garden and disturbed her plants. And a man once called the police to report that the blimp had just flown down his street and had knocked down all the television antennas. Whatever it was he saw, it wasn't the blimp.

Lightplanes in an area where a blimp is flying are drawn to it like moths to a lightbulb. They circle the blimp endlessly, sometimes to take pictures, sometimes just for fun. They waggle their wings, wave through windows, shine flashlights — anything and everything. Of course, the sheer size of the blimp makes it difficult to judge its distance so most lightplane pilots think they are much closer than they actually are. The blimp is also a lot nimbler than many pilots believe, and it can

Above: Some of Goodyear's guests aboard the Columbia. Below: fence-hangers get a close-up view of the Mayflower's takeoff at Newport, Rhode Island.

turn inside almost any airplane ever built, a fact that surprises many of the pilots who buzz the blimp with vague notions of out-maneuvering the big bag.

Air-traffic controllers are apparently so jarred by encountering such a strange object in their bailiwick that they lose their crisp, businesslike staccato and start aw-geeing like kids, gushing questions about speed and range, requesting rides for themselves and their families. It's not unusual for a slow-moving blimp to be used by the tower as a reporting point for incoming aircraft ("Bonanza nine-three victor, report abeam of the blimp on downwind." "Uh . . . nine-three victor, say again please?")

One day, when the *Columbia* was headed inland for Arizona, it began to approach its pressure height, the altitude beyond which it cannot rise without valving helium. The pilot determined that the airship would clear a pass in the mountains on course ahead, but not by much. The *Columbia* nudged into the pass less than a hundred feet above the pavement of an interstate highway, just as a long-haul trucker topped the grade coming in the opposite direction. Nobody on the crew has yet found the words to describe the expression on the driver's face when the whole scene finally registered. They do know he parked the truck for a long while.

On an approach to an Oregon airport in a thick fog, the *Columbia* was proceeding over the water to an instrument landing. Suddenly, out of the gloom, the pilot spotted a fishing boat below. He hit the prop reverse and howled to a halt, opened the window, and asked the fishermen on the deck below, "Which way to Mexico?" Every one pointed dead south, mouths open, knees limp.

The blimp and its crew are blessed with a freedom from the humdrum. Sometimes that blessing is mixed, but there are times when the job is an unalloyed privilege. One such occasion was the flight with a five-year-old with leukemia whose prognosis was as bad as a prognosis can be. Frank Hogan, then chief pilot of the *America,* put the little girl at the controls and helped her direct the big airship. "Grandma, I drove it," the little girl squealed.

Later, they asked what her greatest thrill had been. There was no hesitation. "The balloon," she said. She couldn't know, but almost everyone who has shared the experience would agree.

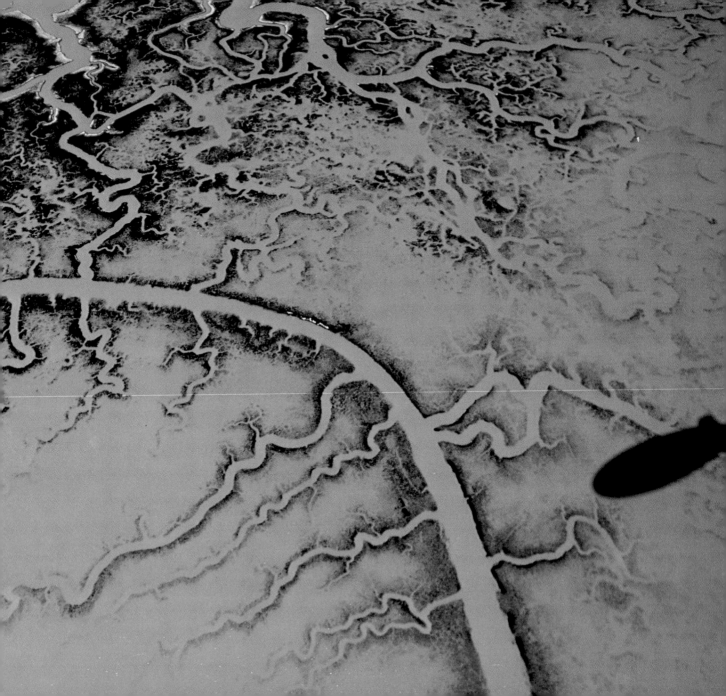

SAILING
LOW

Humans are thinkers in linear measure, their minds happiest with forms arranged in tidy geometrics. (New minitrucks at a Savannah, Georgia, storage lot. Right: Mothballed World War II merchant ships in Suisun Bay, California.)

Overleaf: Water must be the most indecisive of substances; it can't seem to make up its mind about the best direction to take during its trip from high to low. (The blimp's shadow crosses a tidal flat on San Francisco Bay.)

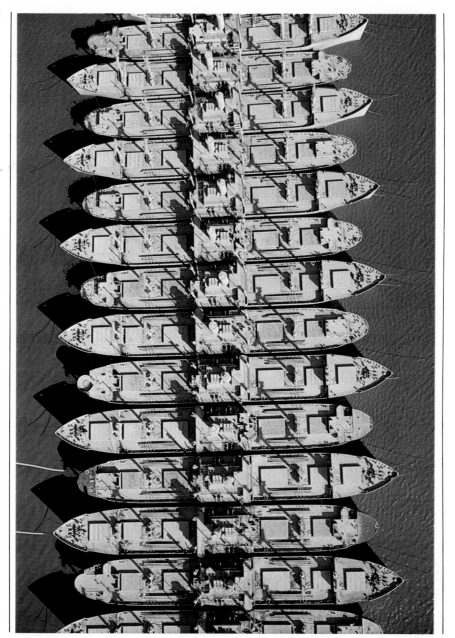

Corduroy rows of soil and crops lie this way and that, large squares with trees and walls to glue their joints. (The paintworks of autumn splash down on rural Indiana.)

The world is never the same once you have viewed it from a few hundred feet. You see as an angel sees, from the vantage of a proximate heaven. It is a startling sight: the ordered impositions of humankind overlying the flowing, textured world of creation. (Log booms in the Fraser River, Vancouver, British Columbia.)

Populations crowd together as if they were poured from a huge bucket, spilling out to coat the world in splashes of color. In the blimp, you see with the vision of one who is too close to a screen: sometimes you get the whole picture, sometimes merely lines or dots, splotches of color which, from a more distant vantage, would create a very different image. (Goggle-eyed bathers watch the America float past a Connecticut beach.)

Unlike the subtle and random textures of nature, man's works are a mosaic of order scaled to please less cosmic eyes. We are the slaves of purpose and plan, weaving tapestries of logic, numbering without counting, our world reduced to columns and rows.

The highway, an
expression in
concrete of our
roving urge, is far
more impressive
from above. Its
long sweeping ribbon
speaks of motion
and speed.
(Coastal Highway 1
near Half Moon Bay,
California.)

Machines and
structures are
studies in knife-edge
lines and inter-
sections. Look down
at the anatomy of
our self-made world:
organs and arteries
of metal, tough
and tempered.
(La Guardia Airport,
New York City.)

Bright strands of steel stretch like a nerve laid raw, the fibers glistening under the polish of passing wheels. (A marshalling yard in Louisville, Kentucky.)

You escape the hard, etched city for the sweet melodies of the meadow and the country lane. Here wheels go softer in the dust and a breeze toys with a grove. The underbellies of the leaves wink pale green and happy, like puppies begging a rub. (An Amish buggy and farm near Lancaster, Pennsylvania.)

Are we anonymous codes in a webwork of beaded huts? The family, the tribe, the town, the nation – overall, a background din through which we strain to hear some hint of who we are. (The houses of Daly City, California.)

The palette knows no end of variety, matching colors of water with those of rock and dust until we're no longer sure what lies below us. (Salt ponds in San Francisco Bay.)

7

44
QUESTIONS
MOST
OFTEN
ASKED
ABOUT
THE BLIMP

1

How can I get a ride on the blimp?

Rides on the Goodyear blimps are available at the invitation of the company only, and they are allotted by the District Manager of the area in which a blimp is operating. Most of the lucky riders are Goodyear customers, local dignitaries, or members of the press. A limited number of rides are made available for a fee to the general public, but only on the *Mayflower* and only when it is at its Miami base. Rides are assigned on a first-call-first-served basis; the price is $7.50 for adults and $5.00 for children.

2

How many Goodyear blimps are there?

There are four: the *Mayflower,* based in Miami; the *America,* based in Houston; the *Columbia,* based in Los Angeles; and the *Europa,* based in Rome, Italy. Goodyear has operated as many as eight at a time since its first commercial ship, the *Pilgrim,* flew in 1925.

3

Are there any other airships in the world?

There is one other blimp flying in Germany; it is owned by an aerial advertising firm, and it is similar in size to the Goodyear ships. This firm is also reported constructing a larger experimental nonrigid with funds supplied by the government of West Germany.

4

Doesn't the Navy have a blimp fleet?

The Navy used blimps for anti-submarine patrol duty in World War II, and as radar picket ships in the fifties, but it decommissioned the last of its lighter-than-air fleet in 1962.

5

What are the blimp's dimensions?

The Goodyear blimps come in two sizes: the GZ-19 size (the *Mayflower*) is 160 feet long, 51 feet in diameter, and 58 feet high, with 147,300 cubic feet of helium. The longer and slimmer GZ-20 size (the *America,* the *Columbia,* and the *Europa*) is 192 feet long, 50 feet in diameter, and 59 feet high, with a volume of 202,700 cubic feet.

6

How much does the blimp weigh?

Without any lifting gas, the empty ship weighs about 12,000 pounds. Inflated with helium it weighs only 100-200 pounds, depending on the amount of fuel, payload and ballast aboard.

7

Would a fire make the blimp explode?

Unlike the great German zeppelins of fifty years ago, the Goodyear blimps are filled with helium, an inert gas which doesn't burn. Although hydrogen is a better lifting gas, lighter and more plentiful than helium, it is terribly flammable, even explosive. Helium is found in the earth, mixed with other natural gases. The most significant deposits yet discovered are in northern Texas, Kansas, and Colorado.

8

Exactly what happened to the "Hindenberg"?

While the huge German zeppelin was making a landing at Lakehurst, New Jersey, on May 6, 1937, a fire started in the tail and within seconds the ship's six million cubic feet of hydrogen were ablaze. The airship was totally destroyed and thirty-six passengers and crewmen were killed. The fire might have been touched off by static electricity, or it might have been an act of anti-Nazi sabotage. The truth will probably never be known.

9

What happens if the blimp gets a hole in it?

The gas in the blimp is at low pressure, so the ship could sustain a surprisingly large gash and still maintain its shape long enough to land. But since there is no internal structure inside the envelope, the gas would eventually escape and the blimp would be as flat as a child's balloon.

10

What happens if the ship loses power in both engines?

The chance of that happening is infinitesimally small. But if it did, the pilot could fly the ship as he would a free balloon, gradually valving off helium to let the blimp down. If just one engine should fail, the blimp can easily fly and maintain ballonet pressure on the other one.

11
Why is the "America" sometimes referred to as the "ghost blimp"?

Early in World War II, the Navy blimp L-8 left Moffett Field in California on a routine anti-submarine patrol flight over the Pacific. Two Naval officers, Lieutenant Cody and Ensign Adams, were aboard. When L-8 had been out for about an hour, Cody radioed that they had spotted an oil slick and were investigating. Then nothing. This message was the last ever heard from the two men.

Later that same day, the blimp was spotted nudged against a cliff on a beach south of San Francisco. As rescuers approached, the ship dislodged itself and drifted inland. It floated down in Daly City, made a perfect landing on its one wheel, and came to a stop in an intersection.

No one was aboard the L-8, and no one has even been able to account for the disappearance of Cody and Adams. The throttles were at idle, everything was working normally, there was fuel in the tanks and the cabin door was open. Some local volunteer firemen slashed the envelope, completely destroying it, in the mistaken belief that the crew might be trapped inside. Only the car was saved.

This car, designated C-64, was refurbished after the war and is now in service on the Houston-based *America.*

12
What is the blimp made of?

The Goodyear blimps are fabricated by Goodyear Aerospace at the company's Litchfield Park, Arizona, facility. They are made of Dacron fabric coated with neoprene rubber. They look shiny and metallic from a distance, but they are actually soft and flexible.

13
How often does helium have to be added?

The ships lose very little helium in normal operations, although the gas does have to be purified about once a year by a distilling machine. As the envelopes age and start becoming slightly porous, the crew might have to add 10,000 cubic feet of gas per month. They buy the gas along the tour and add it as needed since none is carried along.

14
If the ship doesn't let off helium, how does it come down?

Inside the envelope are two air chambers called *ballonets,* one forward and one aft. They can be pumped up with air from the outside or allowed to deflate as the helium expands and contracts. Since air is heavier than helium, inflating or deflating the ballonets will add or subtract weight from the nose or tail, thus trimming the ship. Using the ballonets, the ship can sail up or down in the ocean of air and maintain its proper envelope pressure without having to drop ballast or valve off helium. The two hanging scoops behind the propellers are air intakes for the ballonets; the props force air into them when the pilot opens them up. When the ship is on the ground and the engines are off, auxiliary electric blowers automatically maintain the proper pressure in the ballonets.

15
Could the ship somehow get loose from its mast and float away?

The hitching mechanism is designed to anchor the blimp in extremely strong winds, and failure is very unlikely. Should the ship somehow break its mooring, a zipper-like rip panel at the top of the bag, which is tied by a rope to the mast, would tear the envelope open as the blimp moved away. The resulting gash would deflate the hapless blimp before it could fly very far. The automatic rip panel is a necessary safety feature on all blimps.

16

How is the ship anchored when it's on the ground?

At the very tip of the blimp's nose is a steel ball much like an automobile trailer hitch. This ball locks onto a cup at the top of the portable mooring mast, which is taken along and set up wherever the ship is operating. The blimp is anchored to the earth only at this one point, so it is always free to rotate 360 degrees around the mast as the wind changes. This arrangement has held the blimp in hurricane-force winds on more than one occasion. The blimp will always point itself into the wind, like a weather vane.

17

What are those two ropes at the nose?

The nose lines are used to hold the ship's nose into the wind while it is being handled on the ground. The ship has so much sail area that it will become dangerously unmanageable if it is allowed to get off-wind, so two groups of three crewmen grab each line as the ship lands, run to the sides, and hold the ship into the wind at the direction of the crew chief. The ropes are allowed to hang down when the ship is flying, since there is no particular reason to tie them off.

18

What are those little round bags for?

They are ballast bags, each filled with twenty-five pounds of lead shot. They are put in or taken out from a little compartment at the rear of the car to give a final trim before take-off. The crew chief and the pilot calculate the weight of fuel and payload (including passengers), then add or subtract shot bags as desired. Pilots usually like to take off about "four bags down", or 100 pounds heavy.

19

Why does the crew chief hold up that butterfly net when the blimp lands?

That's a little portable wind sock, and it gives the pilot a final check on the wind direction as he makes his approach. The airship must land directly into the wind. If there is a last-minute wind shift, the pilot will see it in the sock, hit the throttles, and make another go-around.

20

Does Goodyear build its own blimps?

Yes, indeed. The envelopes and other components are fabricated by Goodyear Aerospace, and final erection takes place at the airship hangar in Houston. It takes twenty-five men six weeks to put everything together. Each ship has to be rebuilt with a new envelope every six years or so. The gondolas, however, are just refurbished and put back in the air. Most of them date back to World War II and before.

21

How many lights are there on the sides?

There are 3,080 on the smaller GZ-19 *Mayflower* and 7,560 on the three GZ-20's. The lights are actually auto tail-light bulbs, covered with red, yellow, blue and green plastic discs.

22

How does the night sign work?

Goodyear calls it the Super Skytacular, and they keep the details of its operation under their hats. Basically, it's a complicated electronic system which reads impulses on a magnetic tape and sends out thousands of commands to turn the right lights on and off at the proper instant. The tapes are programmed by computer at the Goodyear Aerospace Night Sign Laboratory in Akron, usually by two wizards named Joe Prinzo and Harold Nixdorf. They can make the sign say or do practically anything.

23

What kinds of engines do the blimps have?

There are different power packages on the two types of blimps. The Mayflower is powered by two Continental GO-300 engines, carbureted, geared down to produce a prop speed slower than the shaft speed, and turning up 175 horsepower each. The larger GZ-20's carry two Continental IO-360's, fuel-injected, non-geared, and producing 210 horsepower each. These are the same engines as those used on a Cessna Skymaster 336. The propellers are pusher Hartzells, constant-speed and reversible. They are custom-made for the Goodyear blimps.

24
How fast and far can the blimp go?

The usual cruising speed is thirty-five miles per hour; all-out top speed is fifty-three miles per hour. That's if there is no wind. A head or tail wind can just be added or subtracted in simple arithmetic. In other words, a thirty-five mph headwind is going to result in a ground speed of zero, but that same wind on the tail will scoot the bag along at a breathtaking seventy miles per hour. When the wind gets much above twenty knots the ship is usually put on the mast until the weather calms. Wind won't hurt the ship in the air, but she becomes very hard to handle on the ground. As to cruising range: the ship can carry enough fuel to fly for twenty-four hours, although it rarely does so. When traveling cross-country (remember that the blimps fly wherever they go, regardless of the distance) the crews try for an eight-hour day, or about 300 air miles.

25
What avionics do the ships carry?

All Goodyear blimps are FAA-certified for IFR (Instrument Flight Rules) flying, day or night. They carry two Collins 360-channel navcom radios, the usual lightplane instruments, digital radar for keeping an eye on thunderstorms, transponder for radar identification, and a couple of instruments peculiar to blimps: manometers for watching envelope pressure and a helium-temperature gauge. As aerial navigation is a bit more complex in the crowded skies of Europe, the *Europa* also carries ADF (Automatic Direction Finder), dual DME (Distance Measuring Equipment), and glide slope/localizer. It also has a fancy little cassette tape machine which announces pertinent facts about the ship in any of ten languages.

26
Is there a kitchen or bathroom on board?

No and no. The pilots usually take a picnic lunch along on cross-country flights, the junior man having to take care of the grocery shopping. There is a relief tube for the men, but the ladies are in for a tough time on long trips.

27
What is a blimp worth? Are they for sale?

Since Goodyear builds them one at a time, it is very difficult to put a price tag on a Goodyear blimp. They're probably worth about $2.5 million each. Goodyear makes them only for use by their own public relations department.

28
How many crewmen and pilots are there for each ship?

The usual complement is seventeen crewmen (riggers, engine mechanics, ground handlers, and electronic technicians), five pilots, and a public relations representative. Since the smaller *Mayflower* is easier to handle, it can get by with a crew of twelve plus the same five pilots and one PR man. Crewmen also share driving chores in the bus and truck, and they take turns standing watch over the ship which is never, never left alone.

29
How do the pilots learn to fly blimps?

Since the pool of qualified airship drivers is limited, to say the least, Goodyear has little choice but to train its own pilots. All Goodyear LTA pilots are also certified as instructors, and they share teaching duties when a new man is assigned to one of the operations. Openings don't come up very often, and there are always hundreds of applications on file. Goodyear only takes applications from fixed-wing pilots who already have commercial, instrument, and multi-engine ratings. A college education is also a big bonus for an applicant.

30
How do the other crewmen get their jobs?

Again, experienced blimp people are hard to find, except in the case of mechanics since the blimps use regular lightplane engines. Many of the permanent crewmen originally worked as part-time "field wage" hands during the winter off-season. The jobs seem great, and they really are a lot of fun, but they're not for everyone. The blimps spend between six and eight months a year on the road, and that can quickly turn into a monotonous blur of motel rooms for a person who doesn't truly love to travel. Many of the men have families and bring them along for the summer tour.

31
What does it cost Goodyear to operate a blimp for one year?

The annual budget is over one million dollars per year per ship, including payroll, equipment depreciation, travel expenses and maintenance. In Europe, where everything from fuel to hotel rooms is more expensive, the cost is double.

32
What does Goodyear get in return for such a huge outlay?

The end result is corporate-name recognition and goodwill. Independent research has demonstrated that people are excited by seeing the blimp and are able to remember exactly when and where they saw it. Over sixty million Americans get a first-hand look at the three U.S. blimps every year, and millions more see the ships on television. The Goodyear blimps are probably the best-known corporation symbol in the United States.

33
Will Goodyear build big airships again?

Goodyear has no plans in the immediate future to expand its airship operations to include experiments with larger airships. A sizeable contract from either government or industry could change all that, however.

34
Is there a future for big airships?

The great zeppelins of the twenties and thirties were ahead of their time, and many people feel that with advances in materials, weather forecasting, and computer technology large airships could be built today with far greater performance, strength and reliability. Large airships could indeed serve as long-distance cargo carriers and heavy-lift vehicles, and their operational efficiency might prove very impressive. However, the capital outlay that would be required for research, development, and prototype construction would run into the hundreds of millions, and at the present time no entity seems willing or able to fund the effort. It's a subject about which some people get very emotional and unrealistic. It would indeed be grand to see the huge ships flying again, but the hard numbers are standing in the way.

35
How big were the zeppelins compared to the Goodyear blimps?

The *Hindenberg* was the largest, and it was 804 feet long, more than four times the length of the larger Goodyear GZ-20's. Its gas volume was over six million cubic feet, and it had 242 tons of gross lift — enough to carry itself plus seventy passengers, a crew of sixty, diesel fuel for a transatlantic flight, luggage, some cargo and mail, and twenty tons of water ballast that could be dropped in the event of an emergency descent. It was faster, too, cruising at about eighty miles per hour.

36
What is it like to ride in the Goodyear blimp?

It is the flight of dreams, smooth, slow and close to the ground. The cabin windows can be opened on a nice day, and passengers (the ship carries only six) can lean out and wave to people on the ground. You can see the ground in far greater detail than from a plane, and a given point stays in view for much longer, since the ship moves at only thirty-five miles per hour.

37
What is it like to fly the blimp?

The blimp has a life of its own in the air. Its movements are slow and ponderous, and yet it reacts very intimately to air currents and thermals. It takes several long seconds for the ship to respond to the pilot's commands, and as a result good pilots soon develop a sixth sense that helps them counteract the blimp's seemingly aimless meanderings. The control surfaces are as big as barn doors and they are not power-assisted. On a turbulent day, the pilot might find himself jamming both feet onto one big rudder pedal to force the ship into a turn. For the most part, however, the blimp is a relaxing joy to fly. The slow cruise speed is a special treat for a pilot used to fixed-wing flight, since he can gaze out and observe the passing landscape in much finer detail.

38
Is the blimp quiet?

Hot-air balloons which float with the breeze are quiet, but the blimp has two lightplane engines which make a good deal of noise, especially on takeoff. The sound level is not unpleasant, however.

39
Do people get airsick in the blimp?

It's less likely than in almost any other aircraft. On a long flight in turbulence it is possible to get seasick, however, since the blimp will pitch and roll much like a boat. Fortunately, the envelope absorbs the bumpiness on normal flights, and the ride is usually as smooth as can be.

40
How high does the blimp usually fly?

Most flights, whether with passengers or cross-country, are at 1,000-1,500 feet. Goodyear likes to keep the ship close to the ground so that people can see it more easily. It has a maximum altitude, depending on the variables of the atmosphere, of about 5,000 feet. Beyond that height the air gets thinner and the helium expands, causing automatic safety valves to open.

41
Is the blimp safe?

Goodyear has flown passengers in its blimps for over fifty years without interruption (except for World War II), and no passenger has ever so much as scratched a finger. It's probably the safest form of air travel ever devised.

42
How does the television camera in the blimp work?

Goodyear has its own specially designed TV equipment for use in the blimps. The equipment is kept in Akron and shipped by air for installation just prior to a given event. The camera is a small German Fernseh color unit, mounted in a vibration-free gimbal mount. The lens is an enormous Schneider 30:1 zoom. The camera's image is transmitted to the ground by microwave, where a dish antenna and receiver pick it up and feed it to the network. The blimp signal can be put on the air live or taped for replay. Goodyear pilots fly the blimp and the company supplies the TV equipment gratis to the networks, as it has done for years.

43
What events do the blimps cover for TV?

It varies from year to year, but the list is impressive. To date, it has given audiences air views of the Indianapolis 500; the Kentucky Derby; the Super Bowl; the World Series; the Rose Bowl and Parade; the America's Cup yacht races; the U.S. Tennis Open at Forest Hills; and the magnificent Bicentennial Tall Ships parade up the Hudson River.

44
How can we get the blimp to come to our county fair or pea-picking contest?

Each year, the blimps receive thousands of requests for their presence. The complexity of moving the ship slowly around the country means that a few of the requests can be honored. Nevertheless, the ships are on the road every year, and they're always interested in new events to visit. The Public Relations Department, Goodyear Tire & Rubber Company, Akron, Ohio, 44316, will be glad to hear your request.